Disney

STAR DARLINGS

Stellar Style

**CREATE YOUR OWN
UNIQUE STARLAND-INSPIRED
HAIR AND ACCESSORIES**

D1418262

EDDA USA

STAR DARLINGS STELLAR STYLE

© 2016 Disney Enterprises, Inc.

Author: Cynthia Littlefield, Kristjana Jochumsen, Olafur Gunnar Gudlaugsson
Photographer: Gassi.is
Stylist: Magnea Einarsdóttir
Make Up Artist: Helga Saeunn
Hairdresser: Sara Anita Scime
Layout and design: Olafur Gunnar Gudlaugsson
Cover design: Olafur Gunnar Gudlaugsson
Printed in Slovenia

Distributed by Midpoint Book Sales & Distribution

ISBN: 978-194078-736-7

www.eddausa.com

List of Contents

Stellar Looks

Sage

Sage is a first-year student at Starland Academy. She is always optimistic and confident and finds it easy to make new friends. Sage's wish is to become the best wish granter Starland has ever seen!

Sages' style and look

Natural Style: Sage's style would be best described as flowing, carefree and comfortable, complementing her free spirit and friendly nature.

Hairstyle: Sage has long flowy hair that she sometimes braids in two long braids in the back. She always tops her hairstyle off with hair signature star head band.

Favorite color: Lavender.

Clothes: A loose blouse with long, wide sleeves, tight fitting leggings, high socks and boots. Optional are short sleeved maxi dresses and nice sandals to go with it.

Her pyjamas are no-nonsense-comfortable, just some shorts, a tank-top and slippers.

Her formal dress is superbly stylish and free-flowing with elaborate strings and glittering stars.

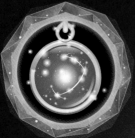

Power Crystal
Lavenderite

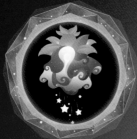

Wish Blossom
Boheminella

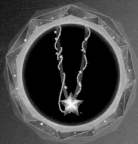

Wish Pendant
Necklace

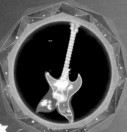

Instrument
Guitar

Leona

The sparkling Leona is in her third year at Starland Academy. She glows with self-confidence and radiant energy and wishes nothing more than to sing and perform on stage.

Leona's style and look

Natural Style: Leona's personality is obviously reflected in her choice of color. Shiny gold and glittering fabrics are the norm for Leona. How else are you going to stand out in the crowd?

Hairstyle: Wild and stylish, with free flowing curls, giving Leona that extra special WOW-effect.

Favorite color: Gold.

Clothes: A golden tank-top, a see-through blouse, glittering capri pants, a wide belt and boots. Optional are long trousers and a warm capelet.

Her pyjamas are equally golden and shiny, but also warm and comfortable.

Leona's formal dress is nothing less than stunning! A long, one-shoulder evening gown with a gorgeous sash at the waist and a flower broach on top.

Power Crystal
Glisten Paw

Wish Blossom
Golden Roar

Wish Pendant
Cuff

Instrument
Microphone

9

Libby

Libby is a first year student at Starland Academy. Filled with the spirit of giving she wishes to become the student body president so she can help everybody get their wish!

Libby's style and look

Natural Style: Libby's generous nature is reflected in her simple yet classical style.

Hairstyle: Finely combed long hair, split sideways on top.

Favorite color: Pink

Clothes: A short, sparkling dress along with a cardigan, tight stockings and stylish shoes. Simple and sweet.

Optional are a short flower dress, leggings and a warm open cardigan. Sturdy boots complete the outfit.

Her pyjamas are a light blouse and trousers worn with a short elegant robe.

Libby's formal dress is a bit more elaborate, styled after her Wish Blossom, the Blushbelle.

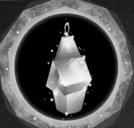

Power Crystal
Charmelite

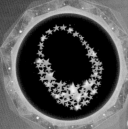

Wish Blossom
Blushbelle

Wish Pendant
Necklace

Instrument
Keytar

Vega

In her second year Vega is laser focused and hard working, a bit of a perfectionist. She wishes nothing more than to be the best student at Starland Academy.

Vega's style and look

Natural Style: Precise, stylish and functional are the key words here.

Hairstyle: Cut short on the sides and top. Exact and stylish.

Favorite color: Blue

Clothes: A long, sparkling jersey with a long, tight jacket with a high collar, tight leggings and designer sneakers.

Optional are a short leather jacket over a long jersey, with a belt in the middle, leggings and warm boots.

Her pyjamas are a functional warm jersey and trousers with comfortable, short socks.

Vega's formal dress is elegantly styled after her Wish Blossom, the Bluebubble.

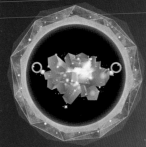

Power Crystal

Queezle

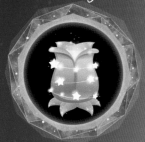

Wish Blossom

Bluebubble

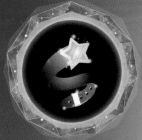

Wish Pendant

Belt

Instrument

Bass Guitar

13

Scarlet

Scarlet has been at Starland Academy for three years. Confident, strong and independent Scarlet has stellar wish-granting potential. She cant wait to go to Wishworld and let her inner light shine!

Scarlet's style and look

Natural Style: Scarlet's rebellious nature is reflected in her radical, independent style.

Hairstyle: Cut very short with a long sidebang.

Favorite color: Black

Clothes: A T-shirt, a hooded jersey, a short sleeved leather jacket, a multi-layered tulle skirt, fishnet gloves, leggings and high, heavy boots.

Optional are a short tulle skirt, a tank top, and fishnet jerseys.

Her pyjamas are a tank-top, soft, short sleeved blouse and capry pants.

Scarlet's formal dress is an elaboration on the multi-layered tulle skirt, with a short sleeved, tight bodice. And the boots stay on!

Power Crystal

Ravenstone

Wish Blossom

Punkypow

Wish Pendant

Boots

Instrument

Drumms

Stellar Accessories

Sage's Hair Band

Sage's free spirit and confidence is reflected in her carefree style. And her hair band would fit perfectly with any hairstyle!

First we need to acquire the silver star. There are all kinds of five-arm-star patterns available in various stores. If you want to create your own stars, be sure to use firm materials that don't crumple or bend easily.

1. Use a glue gun to glue the silver star to the headband. Make sure it's centered

2. Again, with the glue gun, glue the flat resin bead in the center of the silver star. Allow to dry thoroughly.

As simple as that! Sage's beautiful hair band is ready.

Scarlet's Power Crystal

The magical Ravenstone is a complex pattern of dark red sparkling crystals, a beautiful accessory for all Starlings in the making.

1. Put some Mod Podge® onto a baking paper, about the diameter of a quarter. The reason we use Mod Podge® for this project is because it dissolves and becomes transparent, something the glue from a glue gun does not. If you want faster results you can, of course, use a glue gun, but the effect and texture will not be the same.

2. Add an eye pin to the Mod Podge®.

3. Add the crystal faceted round beads to the Mod Podge® and make sure all of them are in contact with the Mod Podge®.

WHAT YOU NEED

Crystal faceted round beads

Black string

Eye pin

Clasp

Mod Podge®

Baking paper

4. Move the eye pin upwards in between the crystal beads.

5. Add Mod Podge® on top of the first layer to make another layer of crystal beads.

6. Let it dry thoroughly – it can take up to 24 hours, depending on how thick the Mod Podge® is.

7. If you would like the pendant thicker add more Mod Podge® and crystal beads on the back of the crystal.

8. Thread a black string or lace through the eye pin and add a clasp or simply tie them together at the back of your neck.

Leona's Wish Blossom

**Leona's Wish Blossom is the golden roar,
an exquisite addition to any fabulous hairstyle**

WHAT YOU NEED

*Assorted yellow
satin cloth*

Small glass beads

Star sequins

Bobby pin

Needle and thread

Glue gun

Trace the flowers, using the template on the right, on various types of yellow cloth and cut them out. Use as many as you want. The different yellow colors are layered from the biggest flower on the bottom to the smallest on the top.

1. Thread the needle with string through all the flowers. Thread 1 star sequin and 1 small glass bead to the string.

2. Hold the star sequin to the top flower and thread again through the star sequin and through all the

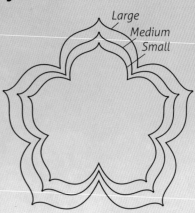

Large
Medium
Small

*Copy the template
to trace the different
sized flower petals.*

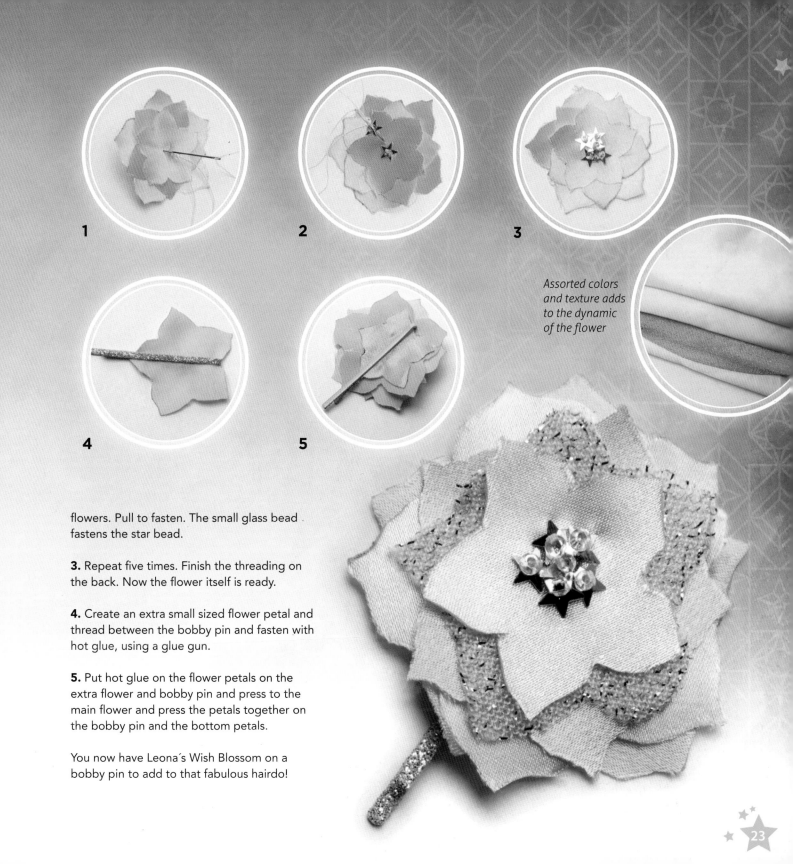

1

2

3

4

5

Assorted colors and texture adds to the dynamic of the flower

flowers. Pull to fasten. The small glass bead fastens the star bead.

3. Repeat five times. Finish the threading on the back. Now the flower itself is ready.

4. Create an extra small sized flower petal and thread between the bobby pin and fasten with hot glue, using a glue gun.

5. Put hot glue on the flower petals on the extra flower and bobby pin and press to the main flower and press the petals together on the bobby pin and the bottom petals.

You now have Leona´s Wish Blossom on a bobby pin to add to that fabulous hairdo!

Star Struck Bobby Pins

Bobby pins are extremely useful for any hairstyle.
But why not take the extra step?
Here is a stellar way to create fantastic
accessories with bobby pins.

WHAT YOU NEED

Small glass beads

Star sequins

Bobby pin

Needle and thread

1.a Cut 14 pieces of threads, 8 inches long.

1.b Take the needle and thread. Make a knot at the end of each thread.

1.c Thread nine glass beads and one star sequin of your choice of color until the beads and stars reach 2 inches, 3 inches and 4 inches.

1.d Repeat as follows:
Five 2 inches long beaded threads
Five 3 inches long beaded threads
Four 4 inches long beaded threads

2. Hold all the beaded threads together and tie a knot so the beads are in line as shows.

3. Take a bobby pin and thread the knot to the end.

4. Hide the knot. If you would like to you are welcome to glue it. Just make sure you do not glue the bobby pin together.

1

Star Struck Hair Combs

Here is a another great way to create fantastic accessories, this time with hair combs.

1. Cut 28 pieces of 20cm long threads.

2. Take the needle and thread. Make a not at the end of each thread.

3. Thread 9 small glass beads and 1 star sequin of your choice of color until the length of beads and star reaches 5cm, 7cm or 10cm.

4. Repeat as follows:

a. 10x5cm long beaded threads
b. 10x7cm long beaded threads
c. 8x10cm long beaded threads

5. Hold 14 beaded threads of various sizes together and tie a knot so the beads are in line as shows.

6. Take a haircomb and thread 1-3 beaded threads into each opening. One bundle to the right and one to the left like picture shows

7. If you would like to you are welcome to glue down the beaded threads to the comb to hold the bundles in place

1

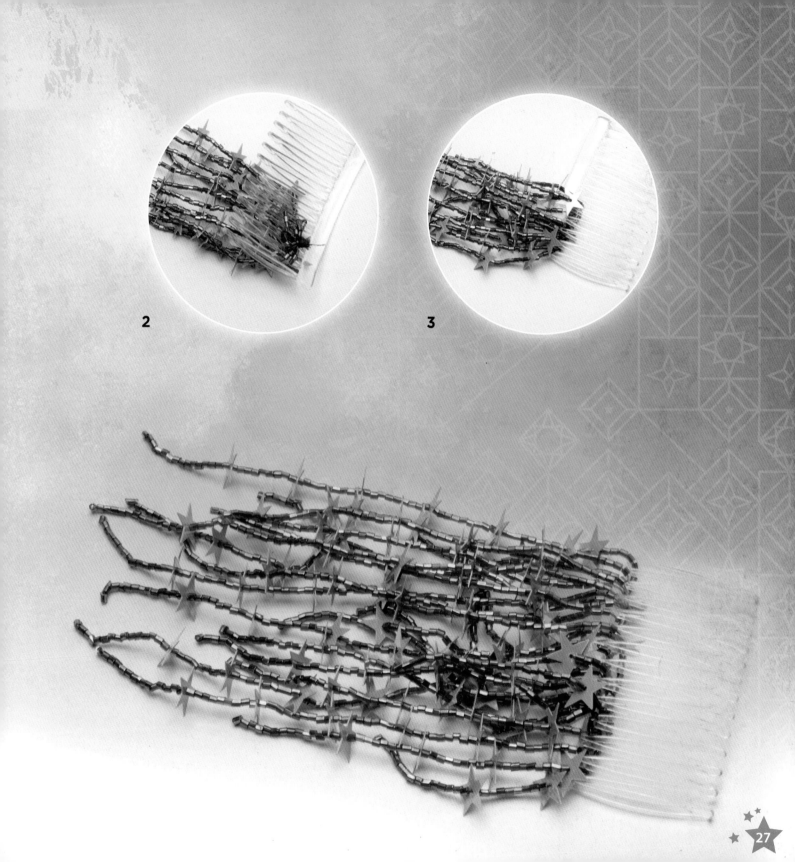

2

3

Vega's Star Decoration

Vega is a bit of a perfectionist, as we can plainly see in this perfect hair comb accessory

First we need to acquire the silver stars. There are all kinds of five-arm-star patterns available in various stores. If you want to create your own stars, be sure to use firm materials that don't crumple or bend easily.

1. Take the comb and one silver star and glue together, using a glue gun. Start from the right.

2. Take another silver star to the left and glue next to the first one with two of the stars arms on or touching the first.

3. Add the third star above but in line with the other two. Make sure all three touch and collide. Repeat with all the stars.

The trick here is to make
an irregular collage of big,
medium and small stars that
collide and touch irregularly.
Play with the form of it.

1

2

3

29

Libby's Wish Pendant

Libby's unique wish pendant is like a constellation of golden stars. Here is how you make this dazzling accessory!

First cut the thin golden metal strings into three segments. First 16 inches long, second 18 inches and third 20 inches.

1. Take the first string and thread 1 golden star sequin and 1 small clear glass bead.

2. Hold the star sequin with your thumb and thread the string again through the hole on the star sequin.

3. Pull tight. Thea glass bead should hold the star and the string in place. If not you can twist both ends of the metal string together under the star bead.

4. Repeat as many times as desired. Use thumbs length between stars and leave 2 inches on each end of the metal strings. Repeat on all 3 strings.

When all three strings are ready it's time to add the lobster clasp:

1. Thread one crimp bead onto the end of all three strings.

2. Place the lobster clasp at the end of all three strings like the crimp bead.

3. Make a loop out of the metal strings and thread them all again through the crimp bead and press it together. Do the same to the other side of the necklace.

WHAT YOU NEED

- Thin, golden, metal string
- Clear, glass beads
- Star sequins
- Crimps beads
- Golden, lobster clasp.

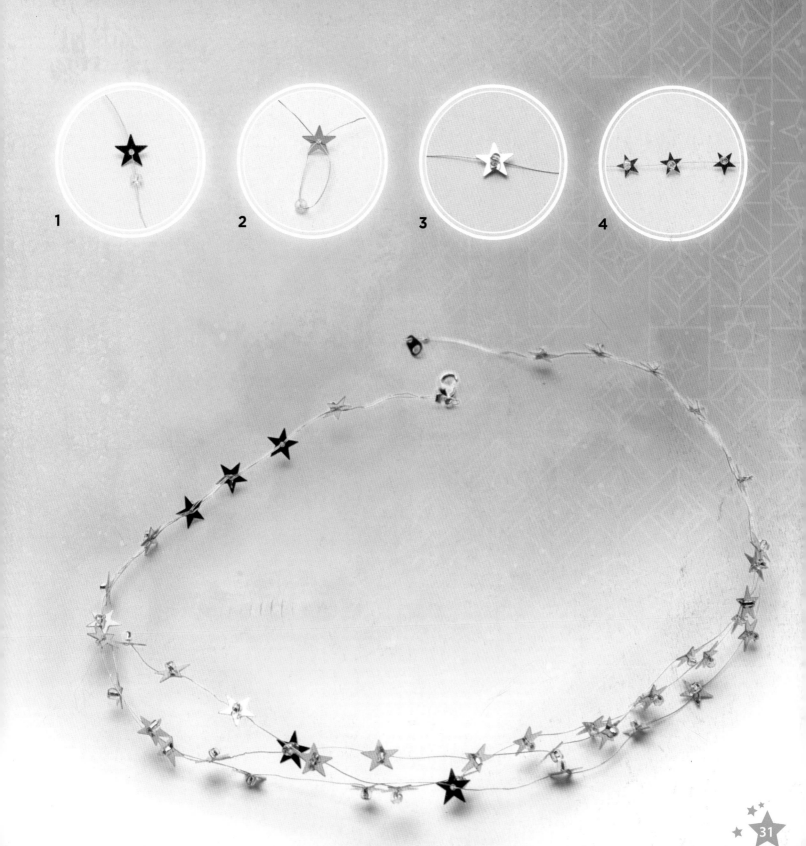

Starling Elastics

Let's face it. Elastic bands are plain. So let's try this fun way to make your elastic bands more stellar!

WHAT YOU NEED

Elastic
Organza ribbon
Flat resin star beads
Glue Gun

The possibilities of this particular accessory are limited only by your imagination. There are numerous different ribbons and star beads to turn any plain elastic band into a great accessory for your lovely hair.

1. First cut the organza ribbon into 10 smaller ribbons, about 4 inches in length. Using a glue gun, fasten the flat resin star beads to each end of the ribbons.

2. Tie a ribbon to the elastic.

3. Tie the remaining organza ribbons to the elastic with equal intervals.

Fasten the beautiful band on a braid, pigtails, ponytail or any other hairstyle that requires an elastic band.

Scarlet's Wish Blossom

WHAT YOU NEED

Silver metal thread
Pink glass beads
Clear glass beads
Silk flowers:
Pink Lily,
Cherry Blossom

The Punkytown is Scarlet's Wish Blossom. Sturdy burgundy leaves cup a burst of creamy star-shaped petals and will enhance any hairstyle

1. Cut a petal of the Pink Lily and remove all excess plastic. Remove all excess plastic from 3 Cherry blossoms. Cut the petals so they look more pointed (see picture 1)

2. Cut 3 metal threads, about 2 ½ inces long each. Add 1 pink glass bead and 1 clear, round bead on each thread. Twist the wire to make a loop with pliers and fasten the pink glass bead in the loop. Hold the

1

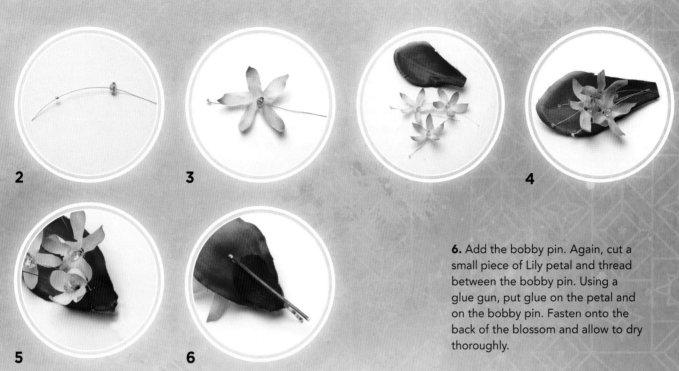

2

3

4

5

6

6. Add the bobby pin. Again, cut a small piece of Lily petal and thread between the bobby pin. Using a glue gun, put glue on the petal and on the bobby pin. Fasten onto the back of the blossom and allow to dry thoroughly.

round glass bead and bend the wires together and twist around two times.

3. While the two wire ends are still together after twisting them, add one Cherry Blossom petal so the clear round bead is in the middle. Spread the wires so they make a line. Repeat with the remaining two.

4. Lay the three combined wires with Cherry Blossom petals on the Lily petal.

5. To hide the wires, cut out an extra piece of petal of the Pink Lily. Glue together, with a glue gun, the three wires and the small petal piece onto the large Lily petal. Allow to dry thoroughly

Starling Hairstyles

Sage's Music Loop Tails

1. Part the hair in the center from front to back to create two ponytails. Fasten each with a hair tie behind the neck.

2. Working with one ponytail at a time, pull a lock of hair away from the rest and wrap it around the hair tie to cover it. Secure the end with a small hair elastic. Lift another lock from behind the ponytail.

3. Loosely loop it around the ponytail.

4. Slip the end of the lock through the loop and gently pull it tight. Use another elastic to secure it just below the loop.

5. Repeat steps 3 through 4 to create two more loops below the first one.

Sage's Braid Wave

1. Clip the hair at the back of the head out of the way. Part the top hair in the center.

2. Brush the loose hair from the left side up and toward the right side.

3. Separate a 2-inch square of hair from the front of the brushed section and weave it into a braid, leaving a long tail. Let the braid fall on the right side of the head.

4. Repeat with a second square of hair.

5. Gather a third square and pull it slightly forward and across the crown. Then braid it on the right side as you did the others.

6. Next, create a second row of braids. Start with the section of hair between the second and third braids. Repeat with the hair between the first and second braids.

7. Create the final braid using the loose hair in front of the first braid.

8. Use a curling wand to loosely curl sections of the unbraided hair, as well as the braid tails.

9. Gently pull the sides of each braid to widen it.

10. Use your fingers to separate each curl into thinner ringlets.

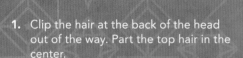

1 2 3 4 5

6 7 8 9 10

Sage's Backstage Braids

11

1. Part the hair at the top of the head in the center. On each side of the part, section off a band of hair near the face and pull it forward.

2. Clip the forward pieces together to keep them out of the way Then section off a square of the hair at the top right side of the head.

3. Braid it and bind the end with a hair elastic.

4. Braid a matching section of hair on the opposite side of the head.

5. Put on the Sage Hair Band, tucking the ends behind the braids.

6. Gather the braids behind the head.

7. Use a hair tie to bind them together.

8. Gather a large square of hair from the upper back of the head (between the braids) and bind it into a ponytail.

9. Pull the ponytail forward over the top of the head.

10. Use large crisscrossed bobby pins to secure the hair near the tie to the top of the head.

11. Lift the loose portion of the ponytail and gently backcomb it over the barrette. Use a couple more bobby pins to secure it. Now divide all the hair at the back (including the braid tails) into two sections. Loosely braid each section, and bind both of the tails together.

1 2 3 4 5

6 7 8 9 10

Sage's Braided Tress Tiara

1. Part the hair at the top of the head in the center. On each side of the part, section off a band of hair near the face and pull it forward.

2. Clip the forward pieces together to keep them out of the way Then section off a square of the hair at the top right side of the head.

3. Braid it and bind the end with a hair elastic.

4. Braid a matching section of hair on the opposite side of the head.

5. Put on the Sage Hair Band, tucking the ends behind the braids.

6. Gather the braids behind the head.

7. Use a hair tie to bind them together.

8. Gather a large square of hair from the upper back of the head (between the braids) and bind it into a ponytail.

9. Pull the ponytail forward over the top of the head.

10. Use large crisscrossed bobby pins to secure the hair near the tie to the top of the head.

Leona's Luminary Locks

1. Divide the hair at the top of the head horizontally. Pull the front half toward the left side and loosely bind it into a ponytail.

2. Pull the back half toward the right side and bind it into a ponytail.

3. Gather a third section of hair from the upper left side of the head and bind it into a ponytail.

4. Remove the band from the front section and divide the hair into two pieces.

5. Loop one piece over the other as if you were tying the first part of a square knot. Gently pull the ends to tighten the knot and then bind them together with a hair elastic.

6. Divide the hair from the second ponytail into halves. Knot and bind them together.

7. Repeat with the third ponytail.

Leona's Pop Star Curls

1. Lightly wet and towel-dry the entire head of hair. Then gather the top section.

2. Brush it back from the face and bind it into a ponytail at the crown.

3. Starting on one side of the head, gather a small section of the hair near the face. (If you make it too thick or wide it won't curl well.)

4. Hold the section away from the head and wrap the end once or twice around a curler clockwise (use small rollers for tight curls or large ones for loose curls). Now roll the curler away from the face and pin it snuggly to the head.

5. Continue rolling sections of hair to create a row that extends to the back.

6. Add a second row of curlers below the first. Roll the hair on the opposite side of the head, followed by the hair at the back. Let the hair dry completely before removing the curlers. Pin back the upper side curls with decorative bobby pins or barrettes.

Leona's Sparkle Rock Band Twist

1. Backcomb the hair at the crown of the head to create a high dome and bobby-pin the base to hold the lift.

2. Stretch an elastic hair band down over the dome and around the head in the same manner you would put on a crown. Pin the band in place.

3. Pull the hair from the top of the head slightly to one side and back over the band. Pin the hair to the band and tuck the ends underneath. Gather a lock of hair from the upper side.

4. Pull the lock back and wind it around the band. Pin the end in place.

5. Continue winding sections of side hair around the band, working your way down to the nape.

6. Next, wind the hair from the other side of the head around the band. Finish by looping the hair at the nape around the band and pinning it securely in place.

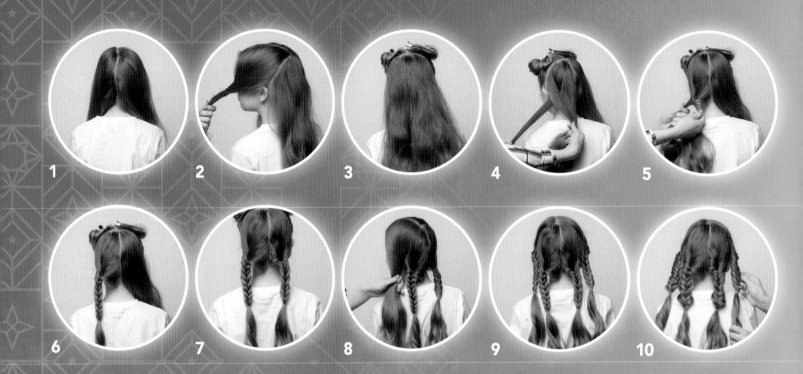

Libby's Braided Bouquet

1. Part the hair in the center from front to back.

2. Part the hair on one side from the crown to the ear. Gather the hair forward of the part and clip it out of the way.

3. Gather and clip a matching section of hair on the opposite side of the head. Brush the back hair smooth and then re-divide it into halves.

4. Divide one of the halves into two sections Add a thick lock from the first section to the second section.

5. Add a similar lock from the second section to the first. Continue weaving the hair in this way to create a classic fishtail braid.

6. Bind the braid with a hair elastic, leaving a long tail.

7. Create a matching braid on the opposite side.

8. Remove the clip from one of the top sections, and weave the hair into a third braid.

9. Create a fourth braid with the clipped hair on the opposite side.

10. Gently pull the sides of each braid to widen it.

Libby's Wishful Waterfall Braid

1. Part the hair at the top of the head in the center. Working on one side, section off a lock of hair near the face.

2. Divide the section into three pieces to begin a waterfall braid.

3. Starting with the left piece, weave the three strands together one time as you would for a regular braid.

4. Add a lock of hair from the top of the head to the new left strand. Then hold the new right strand away from the rest.

5. Grasp a new lock of hair from beside the separated strand to replace it. Now let the separated strand fall loose.

6. Weave the next section of braid as you did the first and, again, let the new right strand fall loose. Continue braiding this way until you reach the back of the head. Bind the end of the braid with a hair elastic.

7. Create a matching waterfall braid on the opposite side of the head.

8. Carefully, remove the hair elastics and bind the two braid tails together. Wrap a Starling Elastic around the band for some sparkly flair.

Libby's Blushbelle Bun

11

1. Brush all the hair from the back of the head up toward the crown.

2. Gather all of the hair at the crown, making sure it is smooth on all sides.

3. Use a hair tie to secure the ponytail close to the scalp.

4. Stretch a bun sponge over the hair tie and lightly pin it to the hair underneath.

5. Let the hair fall over the sponge.

6. Backcomb sections of the ponytail to make the hair to add volume.

7. Spread the hair evenly over the top and sides of the sponge to cover it.

8. If needed, backcomb the ponytail a little bit more.

9. Beginning at the back, wrap and tuck the hair under the sponge.

10. Work your way all the way around. Wind the remainder of the tail around the base of the sponge to hide it.

11. Pin the bun hair down securely.

Libby's Nape Notes

1. Part the hair at the top of the head in the center. On one side of the head, gather all of the hair forward of the ear.

2. Gently pull the hair taut.

3. Twirl the hair clockwise to create a pretty twist.

4. Twirl a matching section of hair on the opposite side.

5. Use a small hair elastic to bind the twists together behind the head. Gently pull the tails apart to tighten the twist.

6. Gather matching locks from the hair just below the first set.

7. Twirl the second set of locks and bind them together as before, lining up the elastics.

8. Again, gently pull the tails of the locks apart to lift and tighten the twists.

9. Create three additional sets of twisted locks, tightening each after you bind it.

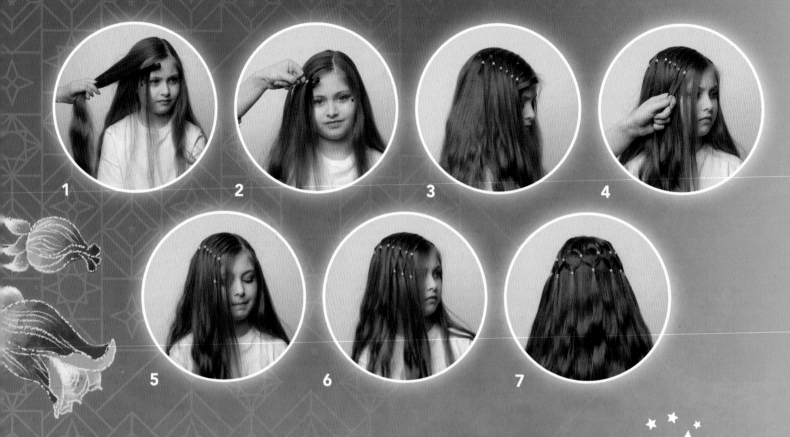

Vega's Bluebubble Bob

1. Starting on one side of the head, separate a thin lock from the hair near the face and clip it out of the way.

2. Lift a second lock to the left of the first and bind it about 3 inches from the top to create a small ponytail. Repeat with a third lock of hair.

3. Continue creating small ponytails all the way around the head so that you have five on each side and six across the back.

4. Divide the first and second ponytails into two sections.

5. Bind the adjacent sections together about 2 inches below the first row of elastics. Let the remaining section of the first ponytail fall loose.

6. Divide the third ponytail from the upper row in two. Bind the remaining half of the second ponytail to the adjacent section of the third. Bind the remaining section from the third with half of the fourth, and so on.

7. Continue the second row of ponytails around the back and opposite side.

1 2 3 4

5 6 7 8

Vega's Guitar String Bling

1. Create a side part at the top of the head. Gather all the hair in front of the ear on the fuller side of the part.

2. Gently twist the gathered hair and pull it back flat against the head. Use the Star Comb to hold it in place, inserting it directly behind the twist with the teeth pointed toward the face. Pin the hair in place behind the comb.

3. Lift a lock of hair from the top of the head behind the comb and bind it with a small hair elastic about 3 inches down from the top.

4. Split the hair above the elastic into two equal sections.

5. Pull the tail of the ponytail up through the opening to twist the hair above the elastic. Repeat to tighten the twist.

6. Create a second twisted ponytail beside the first.

7. Continue making twisted ponytails around the back and opposite side.

8. Decorate each tie with a bit of festive curling ribbon.

Vega's Wish Weave

1. Section off the hair on the right side of the head and clip the rest out of the way.

2. Lift two thick sections of hair near the front of the part and cross the left one over the right.

3. Pick up a third section from along the part. Then cross a new section from the hairline over the section beside it.

4. Weave the same piece under the next section and add it to the third.

5. Pick up a third section from the scalp. This time weave it under the nearest section and over the next before adding it to the third.

6. Continue weaving the hair in this way to create a four-strand French braid.

7. Once you've incorporated all the hair along the face, begin weaving the sections as you would a classic four-strand braid with a long tail. Decorate the tie with a Star Struck Bobby Pin.

8. Divide the loose hair in half horizontally. Use a hair wand to loosely curl individual locks from the lower half.

9. Create a second layer of curls from the hair in the top half.

Scarlet's Drum Brush Shag

1. Gather a large square of hair at the top of the head.

2. Use a small hair elastic to bind it into a ponytail.

3. Bobby-pin the hair on the right side of the head behind the ear.

4. Backcomb the hair on the left side to give it more volume.

5. Bind the backcombed hair into a side ponytail.

6. Gently pull the top ponytail toward the back and loosely pin it in place. Pull the side ponytail toward the top and pin down the hair near the elastic to keep it upright.

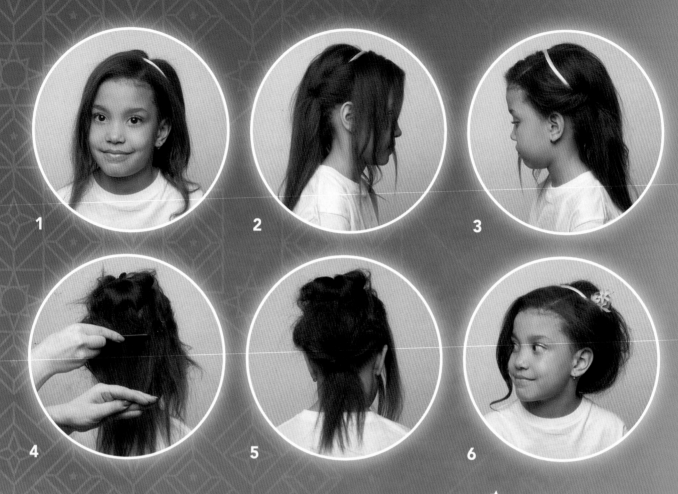

1 2 3

4 5 6

Scarlet's Punkypow Pouf

1. Part the hair at the top left side of the head. Put on a hair band with the ends well behind the ears.

2. On the right side of the head, divide the hair forward of the band into two sections. Leave the front section loose. Bobby-pin the other section over the end of the band.

3. On the left side of the head, bobby-pin all of the hair over the end of the band.

4. Clip the hair at the crown out of the way. Backcomb the loose back hair to add volume.

5. Bind the backcombed hair into a ponytail.

6. Lightly backcomb the hair at the crown, and brush it down over the ponytail. Loosely curl the unbound hair near the face, using gel or spray to hold it, if you like. Bobby-pin a Punkypow Blossom to the hair beside the band.

Scarlet's Snare Drum Do

1. Part the hair at the top of the head on the left. Separate all of the hair above the part and forward of the right ear. Clip the rest out of the way.

2. Divide the loose upper layer of hair near the part into two sections.

3. Lift another small lock from the hairline. Cross it over the nearest (right) section and add it to the far (left) section. Next, cross a new lock of hair from the left over to the right. Repeat.

4. Continue down to the ear in this manner weaving in the loose hair and then finish the tail as you would a traditional fishtail braid.

5. Unclip the rest of the hair. Separate a section at the top and backcomb it to add volume.

6. Backcomb several more sections.

7. Lightly brush the hair back, smoothing the surface.

8. Gather the loose hair along with the end of the fishtail braid into a ponytail at the nape. Embellish the hair tie with a Star Struck Bobby Pin.